Guide to Joomla

I0401459

Practical Guide

V. Telman

Guide to Joomla

1.Introduction

Joomla is a popular Content Management System (CMS) that allows you to create and manage websites easily and efficiently. Thanks to its flexibility and the numerous features it offers, Joomla has become one of the most widely used CMSs in the world, with millions of websites developed using this platform.

Throughout this introduction, we will explore the main features of Joomla, its functionalities, its advantages, and how to start using this powerful tool for website creation.

One of the distinctive features of Joomla is its user-friendly interface. Even if you don't have extensive technical knowledge, you can still use Joomla to create a professional and functional website. The intuitive control panel allows you to easily manage content, images, pages, and much more, without having to write any code.

Joomla offers a wide range of extensions and plugins that allow you to customize your website and add extra functionalities according to your needs. From user management to online store creation, Joomla provides everything you need to create a complete and professional website.

Another key feature of Joomla is its flexibility. You can use Joomla to create any type of website, whether it's a personal blog, a corporate website, an online store, or an online community. Thanks to its modular architecture, Joomla can be easily customized and adapted to your specific requirements.

Joomla also offers a wide variety of responsive templates that allow you to create a website that fits perfectly on any device, whether it's a desktop, a tablet, or a smartphone. This is particularly important today, considering that more and more people access websites from mobile devices.

Another important advantage of Joomla is its active support from a vast community of developers and users. Thanks to this community, you can find useful resources, tutorials, support forums, and much more to help you make the most of Joomla's potential.

Joomla is an excellent solution for anyone looking to create a professional, functional, and customizable website without having to deal with complicated programming procedures. With Joomla, you can create a website that meets your needs and helps you achieve your online goals in a simple and efficient way.

2. Why use Joomla

One of the main reasons why Joomla is so popular is its ease of use and flexibility. Even if you don't have extensive technical knowledge, you will be able to use Joomla to create a professional and well-structured website. The CMS offers a wide range of features and customization options, allowing you to create a website exactly as you want it, without having to write a single line of code.

Joomla has a vast collection of themes and extensions available that will allow you to customize your website according to your needs and stand out from the competition. With Joomla, you can easily change the look of your website with just a few clicks of the mouse and add extra functionality, such as photo galleries, forums, e-commerce, blogs, and much more. These extensions can be installed directly from Joomla's control panel in a simple and fast way.

Another reason you should consider using Joomla is its active and supportive community. Joomla is supported by a large community of developers, designers, and users who share knowledge and resources to help others get the most out of the CMS. There are many online forums, support groups, and educational resources available to help you solve any issues you may encounter while creating and managing your website with Joomla.

One of the biggest advantages of Joomla is its scalability. Whether you have a small personal website or a large corporate website, Joomla can handle sites of any size and complexity. Thanks to its flexible architecture and powerful features, Joomla can be easily adapted to your website's needs, allowing you to expand and update it seamlessly as traffic and content increase.

Furthermore, Joomla is optimized for search engine optimization (SEO), which means you can improve your website's visibility on search engines like Google and increase organic traffic to your site. Joomla offers advanced features to optimize content, meta tags, URLs, and more, to help you rank better in search results.

Another reason you should consider using Joomla is its security. The Joomla development team is constantly working to improve the security of the CMS and regularly releases updates to protect users from cyber threats and vulnerabilities. Additionally, Joomla offers advanced user and permission management features, allowing you to control who can access your website and what actions they can perform.

Finally, Joomla is an open-source CMS, which means it is free to download, use, and modify. This allows you to save money on development and licensing costs and invest more in the design and content of your website. Additionally, being open source, Joomla offers the flexibility to customize the source code based on your website's specific needs, allowing you to create a unique and personalized website.

There are many good reasons why you should consider using Joomla for your next web project. With its ease of use, flexibility, community support, scalability, SEO, security, and zero cost, Joomla is an excellent choice for creating a professional and successful website. If you are thinking of creating a new website or updating an existing one, I highly recommend giving Joomla a chance and experiencing all its potential.

3.Installation of Joomla

Before starting the installation of Joomla, make sure you have all the necessary technical requirements on your web server. Joomla requires PHP (version 5.3.10 or higher) and MySQL (version 5.1 or higher) to work properly. Also, make sure you have access to the control panel of your web server, such as cPanel or Plesk.

The first step to installing Joomla is to download the latest version of the software from the official website, at joomla.org. Once you have downloaded the Joomla installation package, extract it on your computer. You will find a folder called "Joomla" containing all the necessary files to install the CMS.

After extracting the files, upload the "Joomla" folder to your web server using an FTP client, such as FileZilla. You can upload the folder to any location on your web server, but it is recommended to do so in the root directory of your domain (usually public_html or www).

Once the Joomla files have been uploaded to your web server, you can start the installation process by opening your browser and typing the URL of your site followed by "/installation" (for example, www.yoursite.com/installation). You will be directed to the Joomla installation page.

The first screen you will see during the Joomla installation process is the language selection screen. Select your desired language and click "Next" to proceed with the installation.

The next screen is the system requirements screen. Joomla will check if your web server meets all the necessary technical requirements to run the CMS. If all prerequisites are met, click "Next" to continue with the installation.

After the system requirements, you will need

to enter the necessary information for the database configuration. Enter the database name, user, and password that you created from your web server control panel. You can also select the type of database (usually MySQLi, which is the most common) and the table prefix for the database.

Once you have entered all the necessary information for the database configuration, click "Next" to proceed with the installation. Joomla will automatically install the database and configure the settings based on the information you provided.

After completing the database configuration, you will need to enter information about the website, such as the site title, site description, super administrator email address, and super administrator password. Make sure to choose a secure password for the super administrator to protect your site from potential attacks.

After entering all the required information,

click "Next" to proceed with the Joomla installation. The CMS will automatically install all the necessary files and configure the site based on the information you provided. Once the installation is complete, you will be redirected to the Joomla login screen.

Now that you have successfully installed Joomla on your web server, you can access the site administration area by typing the URL of your site followed by "/administrator" (for example, www.yoursite.com/administrator). Enter the credentials of the super administrator you created during installation and access the Joomla administration area.

From the Joomla administration area, you can manage all aspects of your website, such as creating and editing content, installing extensions and themes, managing users, and much more. Joomla offers a wide range of features and customization options to create a unique and professional website.

The installation of Joomla is a fairly simple process that only requires a few steps. By following the instructions provided in this article, you will be able to install Joomla on your web server and start creating your website in no time.

4.Joomla Administration Panel Interface

Joomla is one of the most popular and widely used Content Management Systems in the world for creating and managing websites. Its administration panel is the interface from which you can control and manage every aspect of the site, from content to configuration settings.

The Joomla interface is divided into different sections, each dedicated to a specific functionality of the CMS. Once logged into the administration panel, the user is faced with a main screen that displays a navigation menu on the left and a central area with information and options related to the selected section.

The navigation menu is organized hierarchically and divided into categories such as "Content," "Components," "Websites," and "System." Each category contains submenus that allow access to additional options and functionalities. For example, under the

"Content" category, there are items such as "Articles," "Categories," and "Tags," while under the "Components" category, there are items such as "Modules," "Plugins," and "Templates."

The "Content" section is one of the most important within the Joomla administration panel, as it allows you to create, edit, and organize website content. With the "Articles" option, you can create new content pages, edit them, assign them to categories, and add tags. Additionally, you can manage comments, versions, and advanced settings for each article.

The "Components" section includes a series of extensions that add functionality and features to the website. Among the most used components are modules, which allow you to insert content blocks in various parts of the website, such as the sidebar or footer. Plugins, on the other hand, extend Joomla's functionalities and can be used to add new functions to the website, such as integrating with social media or managing images.

The "Templates" section allows you to manage the website's design, including layouts, colors, and font types used. Joomla offers a range of pre-designed templates that can be customized according to the site's needs, but it is also possible to create custom templates or download templates from third parties to achieve a unique and professional design.

The "System" section contains the basic settings of the website, including general configuration, user management, and security. This is also where you can back up the website, update the software, and monitor the website's performance through system reports.

Another important feature of Joomla's administration panel is the user management system. Joomla allows you to create different levels of user access, so you can assign specific permissions based on the role they play on the site. For example, you can create users with the roles of administrator, editor, author, or reader, and assign them different permissions for content editing, comment management, or access to configuration settings.

Additionally, Joomla offers the ability to create custom user profiles, so you can gather detailed information about each user and personalize their browsing experience on the site.

Joomla's administration panel is designed to be intuitive and easy to use, even for those without experience in website management. The options and functionalities are organized logically, and menu items are described clearly and understandably. Additionally, Joomla provides extensive online documentation and an active user community that can help resolve any issues or doubts encountered while using the CMS.

The Joomla administration panel interface is a powerful and comprehensive tool that allows you to manage every aspect of a website effectively and professionally. With its numerous features and customization options, Joomla is the ideal choice for those looking to create and manage a successful website.

5.Joomla Menu

One of the fundamental elements of any website is the navigation menu, which allows users to move between different pages and sections of the site in an intuitive and simple way. Joomla offers a wide range of options for creating and managing the menu, allowing you to fully customize the site's navigation structure.

Joomla's menu is divided into different levels of hierarchy, allowing you to organize the site's content in a logical and orderly manner. You can define main menus, submenus, and menu items, allowing you to create a complex and detailed navigation structure.

To create a new menu in Joomla, simply access the site's administration area and select the "Menu Management" option from the main menu. From here, you can create new menus, edit existing ones, and organize menu items into submenus and sub-items.

Once the menu is created, you can place it in various positions on the site using Joomla modules. Modules are content blocks that can be placed in different positions on the site and allow you to display the menu on all pages of the site or only on specific pages.

You can further customize Joomla's menu using menu modules. These modules allow you to display the menu in different styles and formats, creating a more engaging and user-friendly navigation. You can use dropdown menu modules, accordion menu modules, tabbed menu modules, and many more.

Additionally, Joomla offers the ability to create customized menus for different user groups. This allows you to create specific menus for registered users, unregistered users, users of a particular group, and so on. This way, you can offer personalized navigation based on the user's profile, enhancing the usability and user experience of the site.

To create a customized menu for a user group, simply create a new menu and associate it with a specific user group. This way, you can offer personalized navigation for different types of site users, ensuring an optimal user experience for everyone.

Joomla's menu is an extremely flexible and customizable tool that allows you to create an intuitive and user-friendly navigation for site visitors. With a wide range of options available and the ability to fully customize the menu structure, Joomla offers the opportunity to create dynamic and engaging menus that enhance the browsing experience and usability of the website.

6. Joomla Modules and Components

Joomla is one of the most popular CMS (Content Management System) in the world and offers a wide range of modules and components that allow users to customize and add functionality to their website quickly and easily. In this article, we will analyze Joomla modules and components, highlighting the differences between them and the advantages they can offer to users.

Joomla modules are small extensions that allow users to display content in specific areas of the website. They can be placed in various locations such as sidebars, headers, footers, etc. Modules can contain text, images, links, contact forms, etc. They can be customized through Joomla's control panel, allowing users to configure module settings and display options.

Joomla modules are very useful for adding specific functionality to the website, such as comment modules, newsletter modules, search modules, social media modules, etc. They can be easily installed through Joomla's administration panel and are compatible with most templates available on the market.

Joomla components, on the other hand, are more complex extensions that allow users to add advanced functionality to the website. They can include custom modules, plugins, and templates, and can be integrated with other third-party components or extensions. Joomla components are often used to create more complex websites, such as e-commerce sites, blogs, forums, photo galleries, etc.

Joomla components can be installed through Joomla's control panel or manually uploaded to the server. They can be customized through the source code or through Joomla's control panel, allowing users to configure component settings and display options.

Joomla modules and components offer

numerous advantages to users who want to customize their website. Firstly, they are very easy to use and do not require specific technical knowledge. Additionally, they are highly customizable and allow users to add specific functionality quickly and easily.

Thanks to Joomla modules and components, it is possible to create a professional and functional website without having to spend a fortune on a programmer or web designer. Furthermore, updates and security patches are regularly released by the Joomla community, ensuring the security and stability of the website.

Some examples of Joomla modules and components include contact modules, search modules, slideshow modules, e-commerce components, forum components, blog components, etc. Each module and component offers different features and customization options, ensuring users maximum flexibility in creating their website.

Modules:

Contact Module: This module allows users to insert a contact form on the website so that visitors can send messages directly to the site owner. The module can be customized with custom fields and set up notification email to receive visitor messages.

Search Module: With this module, users can insert a search bar on the website so that visitors can search for specific content within the site. The module can be customized based on site requirements and search parameters can be set up.

Random Image Module: This module allows users to display random images on the website to make the homepage more dynamic and engaging. Users can set the number of images to display and customize the style of the module.

Components:

Blog Component: With this component, users can create a blog on the website where articles can be published, visitor comments managed, and categories and tags set up to organize content. Users can customize the blog layout and navigation menu.

Online Store Component: If users want to sell products online, they can use a specific component to create an online store on the website. With this component, product management, categories, promotions, and payments can be easily and quickly managed.

Gallery Component: If users want to create a photo gallery on the website, they can use a specific component that allows organizing images into albums and displaying them in an engaging way. Image size, number of columns, and gallery layout can be set up.

Joomla modules and components are essential tools for those who want to create a professional and functional website. With the wide range of extensions available, users can add specific functionality to their website quickly and easily. Joomla is a flexible and powerful CMS that offers numerous customization possibilities, allowing users to create unique and original websites.

7. Creating and editing pages in Joomla

One of the main features of Joomla is the ability to create and edit web pages quickly and intuitively.

Creating and editing pages in Joomla is a fairly simple process, even for those who do not have in-depth programming knowledge. In this article, we will explore step by step how to create and edit pages in Joomla.

1. Creating a new page in Joomla:

The first step to creating a new page in Joomla is to access the website administrator. Once logged in, you can create a new page by following these steps:

- From the main administrator menu, select "Content" and then "Articles".

- Click on the "New article" button to start creating a new page.

- Enter the title of the page in the specified field and add the textual content in the main text box.

- You can format the text using the formatting tools available, such as bold, italic, hyperlinks, etc.

- Additionally, you can add images, videos, or other multimedia elements to the page using Joomla's multimedia insertion tools.

- Once the page creation is complete, you can click the "Save" button to save the changes and publish the page on the website.

2. Editing an existing page in Joomla:

If you want to edit an existing page in Joomla, you can follow these steps:

- Access the website administrator and select "Content" from the main menu.

- Find the article you want to edit in the list of articles and click on the title to open it in edit mode.

- Edit the textual content of the page as desired, using Joomla's formatting and multimedia insertion tools.

- You can also edit the page title, publication date, categories, tags, and other article-specific settings.

- Once the page has been edited, you can click the "Save" button to save the changes made.

3. Using Joomla editors for creating and editing pages:

Joomla offers several text editors that allow users to efficiently create and edit the content of web pages. Some of the most common editors in Joomla include:

- TinyMCE: Joomla's default text editor that offers a wide range of formatting options and basic multimedia insertion.

- JCE Editor: An advanced text editor for Joomla that offers additional features such as image management, custom modules, and more.

- CKEditor: Another popular text editor available for Joomla that offers a range of formatting options and an intuitive user interface.

Individual editors can be installed and customized according to the user's specific needs. You can set the default editor in Joomla's control panel following the instructions provided by the CMS's official documentation.

Creating and editing pages in Joomla is a relatively simple process that only requires a basic knowledge of the CMS and its features. With the tools and text editors available in Joomla, you can create visually appealing and well-structured web pages quickly and intuitively.

8.Adding images and videos, managing categories and tags in Joomla

Joomla is a very popular Content Management System (CMS) that allows users to create and manage websites easily and efficiently. One of its main features is the ability to add images and videos to website content, as well as manage categories and tags to organize content effectively.

In this article, we will delve into how to add images and videos, as well as how to manage categories and tags in Joomla, to ensure a well-structured and easy-to-navigate website for users.

Adding images and videos in Joomla:

Images and videos are crucial elements in improving the visual appearance of a website and engaging users. Joomla allows you to easily add images and videos to website content.

To add an image to an article or page, simply follow these steps:

1. Access the Joomla administration panel.

2. Select the article or page where you want to add an image.

3. Click on the "Insert/Edit Image" icon in the text editor toolbar.

4. Upload the image from your computer or select it from those already on the server.

5. Add alternative text and any attributes for the image.

6. Configure image display options, such as alignment, size, and borders.

7. Once the configuration is complete, click "Insert" to add the image to the article or page.

When it comes to adding videos, Joomla allows you to embed videos from platforms like YouTube or Vimeo. To insert a video into an article or page, follow these steps:

1. Access the video hosting platform (e.g. YouTube).

2. Select the video you want to embed on your website.

3. Copy the embed code provided by the platform.

4. Return to the Joomla administration panel and open the article or page where you want to add the video.

5. Switch to the HTML mode of the text editor and paste the video embed code.

6. Switch back to standard view mode and ensure the video is displayed correctly.

7. Save the changes and view the article or page to verify the video's correct display.

Managing categories in Joomla:

Categories are useful for organizing website content in a logical and structured manner.

Joomla allows users to create and manage categories to facilitate navigation and content search for users.

To create a new category in Joomla, follow these steps:

1. Access the Joomla administration panel.

2. Navigate to the "Articles" section and select "Categories" from the main menu.

3. Click on "New" to create a new category.

4. Enter the category name and optionally a description.

5. Configure advanced category options, such as aliases, metadata, and display settings.

6. Save the category to complete the creation process.

Once categories are created, you can assign them to articles to organize content. During article creation or editing, you can select one or more categories to assign to it, effectively organizing website content.

Managing tags in Joomla:

Tags are labels or keywords associated with website content to facilitate search and categorization. Joomla allows users to add tags to articles to improve navigation and content indexing.

To add a tag to an article in Joomla, follow these steps:

1. Open the article you want to tag in the administration panel.

2. In the "Tags" section of the text editor, enter the keywords or phrases you want to use as tags for the article.

3. You can separate tags with commas to add more than one tag per article.

4. Once you have entered the desired tags, save the changes to the article.

The added tags will be displayed on the article and allow users to click on them to view other related content with the same tag.

Joomla offers users the ability to add images and videos to website content, as well as manage categories and tags to effectively organize content. By using these features, you can create a well-structured and easy-to-navigate website for users.

9. Customizing the layout of the Joomla website

Customizing the layout of the Joomla website can be a complex but rewarding task, as it allows you to create a unique website that fully reflects your personality or that of your brand. In this article, we will explore different options for customizing the layout of a Joomla website, providing tips on how to make the site more visually appealing and functional.

Before starting with customizing the layout, it is important to understand the basics of Joomla and how the site structure works. Joomla is an open-source Content Management System (CMS) that allows you to create and manage websites easily and effectively. One of the main advantages of Joomla is its flexibility and the wide range of extensions available to customize the site.

When it comes to customizing the layout of a Joomla website, there are several options to consider. One of the first things to do is to choose a template that suits your needs. Templates are pre-defined designs that determine the overall look of the site, including colors, layout, typography, and module placement.

There are many free and paid templates available for Joomla, so you can surely find one that fits your needs. Once you have chosen a template, you can start customizing it by changing colors, module layouts, and adding custom graphic elements.

To customize a template in Joomla, you can use the built-in CSS editor or a customization extension like Template Creator CK. These tools allow you to easily modify the CSS code of the template to suit your needs without having to directly edit the source code.

In addition to customizing the template, you can add custom modules to the site to enhance its functionality and appearance. Modules are small graphic elements that can be placed in specific areas of the site and provide additional information or interactions with users.

There are modules for every need: from contact modules to social sharing modules, to product or event display modules. You can search for free or paid modules on the Joomla Extensions Directory and easily install them on your site.

Another option for customizing the layout of a Joomla website is to use template overrides. Overrides allow you to override Joomla's default HTML and PHP code to customize the layout of specific components, modules, or models.

For example, if you want to change how category titles are displayed on an article page, you can create a template override for that specific area and customize the layout to your liking.

To create a template override in Joomla, you need to create a copy of the template files you want to modify and add the custom code to the new file. You can use a text editor or a code editor like Sublime Text or Visual Studio Code to easily make the changes.

Another way to customize the layout of a Joomla website is to use page builder extensions like SP Page Builder or Quix. These extensions allow you to create complex and interactive layouts without having to write any code.

With a page builder, you can drag and drop graphic elements to easily create custom pages. You can add columns, rows, modules, animation effects, and much more to customize the site layout.

Furthermore, you can use the style and configuration options of the page builder to customize the design according to your needs. Many page builder extensions also offer predefined templates that you can use as a starting point for your customization.

Finally, to further customize the layout of the site in Joomla, you can consider using template frameworks like T3 Framework or Gantry. These frameworks provide a solid foundation for customizing the site layout, offering advanced features and greater flexibility.

With a template framework, you can easily modify the site layout through an intuitive interface and customize every aspect of the design according to your needs. You can also take advantage of advanced features such as typography management, mobile device compatibility, and responsive layout creation.

Customizing the layout of a Joomla website offers numerous possibilities to create a unique and visually appealing website. By choosing a suitable template, using custom modules, template overrides, page builder extensions, and template frameworks, you can create a design that reflects your personality or that of your brand.

With a bit of creativity and patience, you can turn your Joomla site into a digital masterpiece that attracts and engages your visitors. Remember to always test the changes on different devices and browsers to ensure proper display and optimal user experience. Customizing the layout of your Joomla site may take time and effort, but the results will definitely meet your expectations.

10. Creating new users in Joomla

Joomla is one of the most popular Content Management Systems (CMS) in the world, used by millions of people to create and manage websites of various kinds. Among its many features, one of the most important is the ability to create new users and assign them specific roles and permissions.

Creating new users in Joomla is a relatively simple and intuitive process, which can be managed directly by the site administrator through the control panel. In this article, I will guide you step by step through the process of creating new users in Joomla, also explaining how to assign them specific roles and permissions.

Step 1: Access the Joomla control panel

The first step to creating new users in Joomla is to access the site's control panel. To do this, open your web browser and type in the address of your site followed by

"/administrator" (for example, "www.yoursite.com/administrator"). Enter your login credentials (username and password) and press "Enter" to access the control panel.

Step 2: Access the "User Management" section

Once inside the Joomla control panel, look for and click on the "Users" option in the main menu. This will take you to the user management section, where you can view all the users currently registered on the site and create new users.

Step 3: Create a new user

Once in the user management section, look for and click on the "New" or "Add User" option to begin the process of creating a new user. You will be shown a form with various fields to fill out to create the new user.

Fill in the required fields, including username,

password, full name, email address, and other necessary data. Be sure to carefully choose the username and password for the new user to ensure the security of the site.

Step 4: Assign a role to the user

One of Joomla's distinctive features is the ability to assign specific roles to users, which determine the permissions and functionalities they can access on the site. During the process of creating the new user, you will have the option to assign a default or custom role.

Common default roles include "Super User," "Manager," "Editor," and "Registered User." Each role has different levels of access and permissions, which can be further customized based on the specific needs of the site. Choose the most suitable role for the new user and proceed with the creation.

Step 5: Save and confirm

Once you have completed all the mandatory

fields and assigned a role to the new user, be sure to confirm and save the changes. You may receive a confirmation message informing you that the new user has been successfully created and is now available to access the site.

The process of creating new users in Joomla is complete. The new user can now access the site using the username and password provided during creation and start using the features and resources available based on the assigned role.

Creating new users in Joomla is a fundamental operation for effectively managing a website and providing a personalized experience to users. By following the steps described in this article, you can create and manage new users quickly and easily, while also ensuring the security and efficiency of your Joomla-based site.

11.Assigning roles and permissions and managing user profiles in Joomla

Joomla is a very popular and versatile Content Management System (CMS) that allows for easy and effective management of content creation and management on a website. One of the most important features of Joomla is the ability to assign roles and permissions to different users of the site, ensuring controlled access to various areas and functionalities of the site.

Managing user profiles on Joomla can be a very important task, especially on complex websites involving multiple users and different user categories. Here's how you can assign roles and permissions and manage user profiles on Joomla.

User roles in Joomla

In Joomla, user roles are predefined categories

that define certain privileges and permissions for site users. The main predefined roles in Joomla are:

- Super User: The site administrator who has full access to all site functionalities and can make global changes.

- Registered User: Users who register on the site and have access to additional functionalities such as submitting comments or participating in forums.

- Anonymous User: Users who visit the site without logging in and only have access to public content.

Additional custom roles can be created in Joomla based on site needs. For example, a "Publisher" role with limited permissions for content editing, or a "Moderator" role with permissions to manage comments and monitor user activities.

Assigning roles and permissions in Joomla

To assign roles and permissions to users on Joomla, you need to access the site's administration panel and follow these steps:

1. Access the Joomla administration panel and click on "Users" in the navigation bar.

2. Select "User Management" to display a list of all registered users on the site.

3. Select the user you want to assign a role or permissions to and click on "Edit."

4. In the "User Groups" tab, you can select the desired role for the user from predefined or custom roles created earlier.

5. In the "Global Permissions" tab, you can define specific permissions for the user, such as editing content or publishing new articles.

6. Save the changes, and the user will now have the assigned roles and permissions.

It is also possible to assign roles and permissions to multiple users simultaneously using the "User Groups" feature in Joomla. You can create user groups and assign them specific roles and permissions to simplify the management of users sharing the same authorizations.

Managing user profiles on Joomla

In addition to managing roles and permissions, it is also important to manage user profiles on Joomla to provide a personalized experience to site users. Here are some tips for managing user profiles on Joomla:

- Allow users to update their profiles: You can allow users to update their personal information, such as name, email address, or profile picture, through their user profile.

- Display additional information in the user profile: You can add custom fields to the user profile to collect additional information about users, such as phone number or shipping address.

- Allow users to manage their preferences and notifications: You can allow users to set their notification preferences or subscribe to newsletters directly from their user profile.

- Display a personalized profile picture: You can allow users to add a personalized profile picture to make their profile more personal and recognizable.

Managing user profiles on Joomla is important to offer a personalized and engaging user experience. By using role and permission management features, you can ensure controlled and secure access to various areas and functionalities of the site, allowing users to interact with the site effectively and according to their needs.

Assigning roles and permissions and managing user profiles on Joomla is a fundamental activity to ensure an optimal user experience and maintain website security. By using the natively integrated features in Joomla, you can easily manage user roles and permissions and personalize user profiles to offer a personalized and engaging experience to site users.

12. How to add functionality with extensions in Joomla

Joomla offers a wide range of features and customizations. One of the most powerful features of Joomla is the ability to extend its functionality through the use of extensions. Extensions are software plugins that can be added to the core of Joomla to enhance its performance and add new features to the website.

There are several categories of extensions available for Joomla, including components, modules, plugins, and templates. Each type of extension has a specific function and can be used to improve various aspects of your Joomla website. Below, I will provide you with a list of the most recommended extensions for Joomla and give you some tips on how to use them to get the most out of your site.

1. Components: Components are the most

powerful extensions available for Joomla. They allow you to add advanced functionality to your website, such as forums, online stores, photo galleries, and more. Some of the most recommended components for Joomla include JomSocial, EasyBlog, JEvents, and Kunena Forum.

2. Modules: Modules are small extensions that can be placed in specific positions on your website to display certain content or functionality. Some of the most popular modules for Joomla include JCE Editor, Slideshow CK, RokSprocket, and SP Page Builder.

3. Plugins: Plugins are extensions that allow you to extend Joomla's functionality in a more targeted way. They can be used to integrate external services, optimize the site for search engines, or improve site security. Some of the most useful plugins for Joomla include Akeeba Backup, JCH Optimize, sh404SEF, and RSFirewall.

4. Templates: Templates are extensions that control the appearance of your website. They determine the layout, colors, font sizes, and other design elements of your site. A good template can greatly enhance the user experience and navigability of the site. Some of the most popular templates for Joomla include Helix, Gantry, YooTheme, and Vertex.

Now that you have an overview of the main categories of extensions available for Joomla, here are some tips on how to use them effectively to get the most out of your website:

- Before installing any extension, make sure it is compatible with the version of Joomla you are using. Incompatible extensions could cause compatibility issues and compromise the security of your website.

- Before downloading and installing a new extension, be sure to read user reviews and ratings. The opinions of other users can provide valuable information about the quality and reliability of the extension.

- Make sure to always keep your extensions up to date. New versions often fix bugs and security vulnerabilities, ensuring that your website is always protected and functioning properly.

- Avoid overloading your website with too many extensions. The more extensions you install, the greater the risk of conflicts and performance issues. Use only the extensions that you truly need and that contribute to improving the user experience.

- Periodically perform a performance analysis of your website to identify extensions that may slow down page loading. Remove unnecessary extensions and optimize the remaining ones to ensure that your site is fast and responsive.

Extensions are an essential element for improving the functionality and performance of your Joomla website. Use them wisely and follow the provided tips to achieve the best results and provide an optimal user experience to your site visitors.

13. SEO Optimization in Joomla

SEO optimization in Joomla is a set of techniques and practices aimed at improving the visibility of a website on search engines like Google, Bing, and Yahoo. Since Joomla is one of the most widely used CMS in the world, it is crucial to know and correctly implement various SEO optimization strategies to achieve positive results and position well in search results.

To optimize a Joomla website, it is important to consider various aspects, such as the site's architecture, content, keywords, meta tags, backlinks, and more. Let's take a detailed look at some of the key steps to follow for good SEO optimization in Joomla.

First and foremost, it is crucial to choose a good template for your Joomla site. The template not only needs to be visually appealing but also optimized for search engines. Ensuring that the template is responsive, fast-loading, and compatible with the latest versions of Joomla is essential to provide a good user experience and achieve a good position in search engines.

Once the template is chosen, it is important to carefully plan the site's architecture. Creating a well-organized and intuitive structure helps both users and search engines navigate the site effectively. Organizing content logically, creating a hierarchy through menus and subsections, and using categories and tags correctly can improve the site's usability and indexing on search engines.

Another crucial aspect of optimizing a Joomla site is choosing the right keywords. Keywords are the terms or phrases users enter into search engines to find information. It is important to select relevant keywords for your industry and strategically incorporate them into the site's titles, content, and meta tags. Using tools like Google Keyword Planner or other SEO tools to identify high-performing keywords can help improve the site's visibility on search engines.

In terms of content, it is important to create quality and original texts for your Joomla site. Search engines reward sites that offer useful, relevant, and unique content to users. Writing interesting, informative, and well-structured articles, using high-quality images, and regularly updating the site with new content are all strategies that can help improve the site's ranking on search engines.

Technical optimization of the site is also essential. In Joomla, it is possible to optimize various SEO settings through the administration panel, such as managing meta tags, URL management, creating sitemaps, and more. Ensuring that all SEO settings are configured correctly is crucial to ensure good indexing of the site on search engines.

Another aspect to consider for optimizing a Joomla site is the page loading speed. Search engines penalize websites that load slowly because good user experience is essential for the success of a site. Optimizing images, reducing unnecessary code, using reliable hosting, and regularly cleaning the database are some actions that can be taken to improve page loading speed.

Finally, building quality backlinks is another important aspect of SEO optimization in Joomla. Backlinks are links that come from other websites and point to your site. Obtaining backlinks from authoritative and relevant sites in your industry can help improve the credibility and ranking of the site on search engines. However, it is important to avoid buying backlinks or using unethical link building techniques, as search engines can penalize the site and push it down in search results.

SEO optimization in Joomla is a complex process that requires time, effort, and specific knowledge. Following all SEO optimization practices and techniques correctly can help improve the site's visibility on search engines, attract more visitors, and increase organic traffic. With a strategic and consistent approach, it is possible to achieve excellent results and rank at the top of search results.

14.Security in Joomla

Security in Joomla is a topic of fundamental importance, as like any other content management system (CMS), Joomla is a fertile ground for cyber attacks by hackers and malicious actors. Therefore, it is essential to adopt adequate security measures in order to protect your website and the sensitive data of users.

In this guide, we will delve into the main threats to the security of Joomla and provide practical advice on how to strengthen the security of your website.

The main threats to the security of Joomla include:

1. Software vulnerabilities: like any other software, Joomla can contain vulnerabilities that can be exploited by hackers to compromise the site. It is therefore important

to always keep your Joomla installation up to date by regularly installing security updates released by developers.

2. SQL injection attacks: this type of attack involves inserting malicious SQL code into input fields of the website in order to obtain sensitive information from the underlying database. To protect your site from these types of attacks, it is advisable to use secure input parameters and properly filter user-entered data.

3. Cross-site scripting (XSS): this is a type of attack that involves inserting malicious code into the website in order to compromise user data or spread malware. To protect your site from XSS attacks, it is advisable to properly filter input data and use HTTPS protocols to ensure a secure connection.

4. Weak passwords: using weak or easily guessable passwords is a serious security risk for any website. Make sure to use complex

passwords, consisting of uppercase and lowercase letters, numbers, and special characters, and to regularly change them to avoid unauthorized access.

5. Unauthorized access: it is important to limit access to the Joomla administration panel only to authorized users, using secure passwords and appropriate user roles. Additionally, it is advisable to regularly monitor user activity to detect any unauthorized access attempts.

To protect your Joomla site from these and other security threats, you can adopt various security measures including:

1. Always keep your Joomla installation up to date by regularly installing security updates released by developers.

2. Use reliable security extensions, such as firewalls and antivirus programs, to protect your site from cyber attacks.

3. Limit access to the Joomla administration panel only to authorized users, using secure passwords and appropriate user roles.

4. Protect the website using security protocols like HTTPS, to ensure a secure connection between the user's browser and the site server.

5. Regularly backup the site's data, in order to quickly restore the site in case of a cyber attack or data loss.

6. Regularly monitor user activity to detect any unauthorized access attempts or suspicious activity.

With these practical tips and security measures, you can effectively protect your Joomla site from cyber threats and ensure the security of user data. Cyber security is an ongoing and evolving process, so it is important to stay constantly updated on new threats and adopt the most appropriate security measures to protect your website.

Index